For my Me and My Parents

I want to thank myself for being most courageous. With me facing my fears, I am free to see what my parents have always seen in me.

I am thankful for the beauty of evolution with the aspects of my relationship with my father, Duane and (Bonus Mother) Shatima Thomas. You both have encouraged me, reminding me of my origin and strength. I am so happy I know you beyond my father and bonus mother.

I am grateful for seeing the beauty in my mother's transition. My mother, Imani Pamoja, you have imprinted me with the gift of writing,.

Your spirit reigns in my heart. I see you in myself.

You live on in your children, grandchildren, and great grandchildren. You are in my dreams, for your dream is my dream...Until we meet again,

Queen Mother, Goddess of Strength.

THE CADENCE OF MY HEART

POETRY BOOK

BY

DR. J BLISS

It doesn’t matter if another person doesn't believe in me. I came into this world solo, and when I exit, I’m certain there won’t be bunk beds where I take my final rest.

Yet, one thing I know for sure, it’s my strength that’s brought me here to birth myself from tragedy.
I am triumphant!

CONTENTS

BIRTH 11:11

I put my heart in the hands of Jack Sparrow

Dancing in the building of love consumed by hate

Trusting him, yet not once did he reciprocate.

I cried out the countless nights of rejection.

I, cut from the side, stabbed in the back, still my blood seeped from my throat.

Without a note of apology for such cruelty

Holding my composure, not releasing the green Hulk in me

I bled

I fled the scene as my roots took hold of me

rebirthing me from the tree of life

Never with the projection that this was a setup to release the brave one in me

These root piercings are ever so accepting of me, demanding me to see the indication of this rejection as a test to find the master key

for my feet were set in
the wrong direction for
protection
connection
affection
To find me

A curriculum designed carefully, intricately, and painfully, including Rejection

my very own pain lesson set to find self
Meet self
Nurture self
Protect self
Connect self
and give the proper affection to self
Finding self through pain
As a woman gives birth.
I was set to give birth to Me

Finding parts never known existed to become better as completion takes place, comprehending myself through pain

With the motive to locate the key master of my safe
My heart, a safe in which only one has the codes
combinations unbeknownst to me

Charting through the simple layers for the code this one attains has the will to pile the intricacies of depths to my soul to meet me on my frequency.

Released to the wild

Boldly, I stand to shut out the pirates attempting to take from me what does not belong to thee

Smacking the very blood, he cut from me; I spit on his face

while my piercing eyes seek out the key master of my safe

the divine one graced upon this earth, bypassing the multiverse of doors opening the depth of

my heart

my soul finding things I knew not existed till the master key holder of my heart presents himself

I remain vigilant, avoiding giving my heart to all Jack Sparrows.

SPIRITUALLY

Are you spiritually underage?
Do you only see me as eye candy?
Can you see me from a spectrum beyond the night?
Do you have the telescopic lens, heavenly, divinely, to distinguish me?
Are you attracted to my fruitful production?
Do you only wish to feast upon me?
Do you have spiritual maturity?
The mind, the will, the emotional intelligence to fathom how to summon fruitfulness from me?
Or do you sit there to contribute barrenness upon me?
Do you crave my soul food which does not touch a plate?
Do you feen for the food of my aura?
Are your optics perceiving my healthy spirit?
Can you sense the energy of purpose multiplying by my mere grace?
Is your soul intelligence electrifying you with cues of

my vines vibrating to branches connected, summoning my fruitfulness?

Or are you as disconnected as the sticks beneath the tips?

ONLY THE SPIRITUALLY MATURE one can see the depth of me, expose, process, and assist in healing my negatives while developing the true image of me.

YOU TAKE A BOW BEFORE ME, silenced unless spoken to.

Are you still there before my personage? You, spiritually immature…

I grant you permission, flee…but be cautious, turn your back not.

The acceptance of barren gifts, heretofore, cease to exist.

1013

You are the catalyst that whisked into my life,
to spiritually unfold deeply rooted layers,
accelerating an awakening process to launch me like a rocket

GRACING your presence was like an energy injection more like
rocket fuel for the soul
exploding my heart open in an unmerciful way, but all from love and for love.

SO AS THE sun rises and falls, it is you I see, your energy I feel.
No longer lost in the illusion of a form of 3D, but catapulted into the energy that awakens my soul
Moving from duality to non-duality

Centering us to the true being
Awakening to truth

FAREWELL to your physical
I honor you, my catalyst
Continuing life with or without the physical sense of you
I thrive, awakening to one conscious of you with energy without separation
Attaching not to form
Voiding the stunt of my growth by wants
Embracing life to flow in and out to my needs

OPEN TO ENERGY, I remain
Removing myself to attachment of from
Open to energy, I am in connection, happy enjoying experiences
Receiving what I need, emerging in love rapidly I unfold, awakening ever more ascending in my divine consciousness energy electrifying me to my higher self
This is true liberation
Dwelling in divine energy
the heart space without hang-ups of form
Free experiencing what comes, cherishing, savoring equally what comes and accepting what must flow to go with each season.

. . .

YOU ARE the catalyst that whisked into my life, to spiritually unfold deeply rooted layers, accelerating an awakening process to launch me like a rocket…

I see
I believe
I am free
I am, finally, me.

DESERVE

I deserve love
I shall have nothing less
one that canopies me
securing me in
made timid by Philophobia yet finds themselves
philosophize and so much more
with me
padlocking their love publicly for me
Filled with romantic gestures, convinced to express amour
promising everlasting love from the LOVLOX bridge in Augusta
beyond the distance, where it's forbidden
at Pont Des Arts bridge
for my love would let no law degrade their love bits, tenderness
determine, constantly defining

'Je t'aime, beaucoup.'
irretrievably wrapped in love with me
as the vines that grow wickedly on the bark of a tree,
impossible to analyze or solve where their vines of love begin or end
I deserve love
constantly growing wild between the flow of wind that does not bend at the end
yet glow with the flow to show with each blow
I'm in this thing for life
not temporarily confined by the condition of compatibility momentarily for evolution requires change
in this here life
that's why I got to be his wife
For the depiction of tall trees falling before me will crush he, hush…he
to live in a mere imagination
without me
I deserve love
me
yes
me
I deserve love as my soul's vibration shines endlessly
attracting the source for he
To glide to the frequency of true purity
connecting to fragments of his soul
in me
energetically, magnetically intertwine, awakening ourselves to be creating our reality
I deserve love

a process that cannot be finished,
loved
love
I deserve love, yes, me!

REALITY

My reality, loving you scares me.

Not to the point that I'm scared to love, but not free to love

When I travel just for a midnight glimpse of you, your lips hit my lips, and sparks fly

When I prepare a meal with you in mind, lost in my femininity

When I gather loose leaves to conjure tea, as the fragrance of each note hit, my mind relaxes, turning my lips up in thoughts of you

When I tell you my dreams, facing the existential thoughts staring into your eyes

When your touch falls upon my skin, my heart circuits

When I look in your eyes, ready to say I love you, a cyclone rotates counterclockwise without butterflies in my head

Shouts reach my ears, desist, the second I'd jump out of the airplane to fall, abstain, I hear.

. . .

My reality of loving you scares me.

Not to the point that I'm scared to love, but not free to love

When I leave your presence, I feel mindless, knowing we have two different long-term wishes

You cover yourself from your fears while I embrace my fears to love

I love with my everything, but with you, brakes appear like I'm urgently crashing in the fast lane

Loving you scares me.

Not to the point that I'm scared

Loving you scares me because of pauses, screaming I can be me temporarily

with persistent reminders, we have two different end games

Yours that's free to flow until the river hits upon the bank, impacting the evaporation of such love to exist

Mine that's free to flow, surpassing the span of the Nile River

Flowing the distance for light not to penetrate, deeper than the depth of the Congo

My reality is loving you, not me loving me, yet ceasing me from being free

to breathe

to be me

Unapologetically

That…that is my reality.

NEW

With the grace of a woman, I release you.
I let not the grief of a child whirlwind inside of me
Interfering,
detouring me on my path to my divine destination
Thank you for gracing me with your presence each yesterday, but I see no reason to grieve chaos for my today; my tomorrow chooses the calmness of the river
Distance over disrespect
naturally, in times of stress, you've seen me uncomfortable between the old layer and new skin to be
but
I'm still growing, you see, removing parasites in my shedding
leave me be,
there will be evidence; you will still feel me
yet let me be as I ascend
waiting not, I've planted my garden, decorating my soul

instead of awaiting your entrance of someday, someway, someone brings me flowers

My today is under construction, building the road from the uncertainty of tomorrow's ground my tomorrow places me at an opportunity before my future opportunities

As I've learned my level of endurance, the strength of my ancestors resides in me

my worth

my value is incalculable

You wish to leave? I wish you well as I dance upon the foliage falling before my feet

I recognize the daylight change as the temperature alters the process of leaves stopping while the green disappears, opening the vibrant yellow to orange, yes, the futures fall in mid-flight escorted by their fall splendor

I'm not bogged down with bitterness, heartbrokenness

yet embrace nature

falling in love between each wind

I embrace nature cascading upon my skin

embracing my journey

open mind

open heart

opening my energy to step forward, entering the canopy

Moisturizing my feet beyond the forest floor as precipitation falls upon my lips to my hips, the absence of wildfire leaves me to position for no escape

I am free

wet

warm

consistently taken by no seasons, learning my endurance

the strength of my ancestors is within me

my worth

my value is incalculable

learning, learning taken by the breath of freshness of life encapsulated by evergreen trees energized by the power of such a natural terrestrial ecosystem

taken by no seasons, for every goodbye has filled me

with

learning, learning, learning

I grant permission for this energy to transfer

Changing form, rearranging deeply between my toes, tingling sensations crawling from my feet to the entanglements of my legs, between my wetness

Falling upon my engorging lips, gripping at my hips

this energy flows

grounding me, securing me, bursting further through my crown

moans, yells, screams…

I have a new canvas before me

new

new

Finally NEW!

CHANCE

My greatness didn't manifest by happenstance
my existence delivered with my stand
operating in my purpose, purposely *Not By Chance*
my greatness didn't manifest by luck
my existence delivered with my pen operating on purpose, purposely Taking Chances
my greatness manifestation
began knowing I'm heaven-sent
my existence assisted by the descendants of my ancestors operating in my purpose, purposely with the exception this might be my *Last Chance*
my greatness manifestation is beyond an anomaly
I believe in me, my existence strengthened by the goddess within *Breaking* Out In *Dance*
no longer trapped by the highs and lows of *Night and Day*
I'm standing on purpose

I am my greatness, greatness I am,
my existence delivered with my pen; there's *No Chance*
for I am greatness, greatness am I
I am Chance.

TRUST

Have I still not earned your trust? I recognize I surge more than butterflies in the midst of your day, flowing through out your body I sense the strength growing before you with my presence. Yet, you question me, my presence, my being. I'm not some little fling.

You come before me asking me to trust you when what I hear is…if I shall fall you volunteer to protect me from such fall. I hear if I think I'm going to fall, trust in you, for I will not.

Yet, I still ponder…have I still not earned your trust? Have you not noticed my strength doesn't yell for protection for I can easily be an abyss with floodwaters engulfing all land.

. . .

I WANT to be the lullaby that calms you,
centers you,
surging peace when you are before the raging storms
Calming you to the state of your most upright polite mannerisms where not a blemish could be found
I'm not only interested in your love language for I'm more than a friend seeking the melody of tranquility as a serene stream escorting you with me before the peace language where no hypertension exists only the tension of waves of friction from our chemistry where we can be… peace beneath the core of the monster of a protector I know you to be
Peace
As I give you ease just as you, please to protect me, respectfully
I bid to you my protector whilst I deserve respect, allow me to be your invisible protective field that only you feel
Have I not earned your trust, proven capable of such responsibility for it shall set a liability dividing me from being more than one you trust, sexually escorting you, spiritually. I sense the hurricane has taken the breath of your lungs as I walk through the door, have you yet not recognized my aura is from a higher elevation?

APPLY trust in me taking me as I am trustworthy
a healer
divine
the one complimentary of your entire existence

. . .

You say trust me as your energy leaps, bounds to protect me

Have you not known why you sleep lately?

Is it too much for you to fathom in me there is no job, yet a career for life?

Do your ears hear the rumble of thunder silenced, shifting to the trickling echoes of streams falling from stone to stone?

Trust, I give not to anyone, for I've learned trust is earned

Yet, with your eyes do you only see a friend dressed in such royalty?

Have I proven capable of your trust?

Can you trust me with your children?

Can you trust me with money?

Can you trust me with love, better yet, your heart?

Can you trust me with the most sacred stories of your being?

If yet these things you cannot trust, for no proof of being applicable, exist for sustaining such trust in the said capacity

. . .

I STAND before you asking you why ask me to trust you?

I DO TAKE you as you are,
Yes, I respect you as noted you respect me

TRUST…
I notice your admiration for me, your care for me
Trust…
I notice my willingness to freely be in my divine state of femininity

TRUST…
I notice you not willing to trust me
Just how do you think I be
And you say trust you, yet least you trust me

I WANT to be the lullaby that calms you,
centers you,
surging peace when you are before raging storms

I'M NOT ONLY interested in your love language, for I seek the melody of tranquility, escorting you with me before the peace language
Peace…just peace in me
Peace.

END

The moment I understand why you hurt me, I become the person that hurt me.
Understanding why you hurt me is equivalent to becoming the one who hurt me.

My family members have done terrible things to me as a child, resulting in that pattern continuing as an adult. I wanted to know why my relatives hurt me, only to enter a relationship duplicating and compounding my hurt as I focused on
'Why hurt me.'

It could and will never make sense because I'm not the person who set out to hurt me intentionally.

Comprehending another violation toward me is not a requirement but moving forward and enforcing boundaries while protecting my peace is my obligation.

I'm a survivor of suicide, loss of my own life because of pain, and unacceptable pain by another that I entered this world without.
No longer with that person,
No longer accepting applications for pain.

When you see me, you don't see the pain, the struggles I encountered…
Yes, I lost myself once and never again.

I present the courage I took to move forward and let go of every violation from childhood to adulthood. I'm giving myself what I'm owed, an apology and permission to live my best life.

Every day I'm the woman of my dreams, unapologetically me!
I stood up for the broken little girl in me and fought for the neglected young girl in me.
I am my biggest shero.
I apologize to no one for securing and loving myself.

. . .

I lost myself once and never again…for
I met myself
and I vow with all my power to love me courageously,
fiercely, and nurture me without end.

HAIL – O

We brace the crowd
Your essence reminiscences my senses
Signaling to me **your** presence.

I twist, resisting as *we* witness the man of the hour,
Glancing upon images, depictions of royalty,
vibrant **energy pulsates** in my ear
And *we* depart, in cheer.

We gallantly lift to the floor designated for the evening.
I speak
Then split.
Your intrinsic nature,
like a cosmopolitan distribution

extends through the space
reaching my habitat through mere soft breaths…

I turn with a prance, met by **your** confident tone and
piercing eyes that follow
to the depth of my soul…
Shutting off the noise…
I step away.

Through the crowd, I move towards the one I'm *vowed* to,
Yet still magnetized by the **force repelling** from the source
of **your** being.

We join in celebration of one dear.
Sitting ***we*** chat, ***we*** mingle, sharing laughs.
An electric current passes through the threshold
Demagnetizing
The field as I speak…it's Inescapable…

I turn
then twist
Your presence forms a compound
an indispensable property,

I know not **reality**…

Inspired, I form words from my dreams,
Still
Know not my **reality**…

I construct my paint
A tale of bliss…
A tale of bliss…

I support artistry, unaccompanied
I perceive the sound of **your existence** with such
intellectual induction.

The nucleus basis ALARMS
Yet I walk to such **fear.**
Extending to greet
tingles map about,
coming to surface the particles
as the attraction of the moon and sun changes the pattern
of the tides.

The acknowledgement of my arrival accompanied with the
stimulation from the depths of **your** eyes produces
chemicals sending me to utterances…with the flick of my
wrist
The tip of my finger presses upon **your** chest to stop the
bouncing of exchanged energy.
I walk away
Yet **your** vocal cords exclaim in my ear
To my soul
Yet I know
not my **reality**…

I face **you** once more
we embrace without words
Worry no more

Rings

Worry no more

Rings
I vent, My tears
F A L L. to my face. A cleansing takes place,
Challenged to identify my emotional landscape
Walking through a lonely maze
My shattered heart reveals
My shattered heart reveals
Your presence heals.

Devising **you're** more like the **truth** of something **deeper** than I could **imagine**…

We EMBRACE and a **brighter** side evokes an **energy** of **protection, Fueling** my **being**,

Signing **our souls**

Beyond the celestial clouds before the Spiritual realms.

Apart my emotions form into a super cell,

Large hail resides inside, as high winds rotate

Your Voice brings forth

Sunshine,

A warmth

Like no other

As the forecast settles

I calm

Enjoying the **Sunshine,**

A warmth

Like no other…HELLO.

GOOD NIGHT

I want to tell you good night.

Not to have the gentleness of your arms embrace me

No,

for when you wrap your arms around me, like caffeine, it wakes my senses

I want to tell you good night

Not to be within your presence

No,

for when you're near me, my heart races, removing all aspects of time and spaces

I want to tell you good night.

My wrestling night will settle, gracing me with tranquility as the calm waterfall replenishes my soul.

I want to tell you good night

As I shut my eyes and meet you in my dreams

I want to tell you good night.

As the words escape my lips
removing from the light
I whisper to you good night
Good night…one day, I will tell you
Good night.

IN THOUGHT OF YOU

To be in thought of you, to feel a warmth of heightened sensations saturating my insides, flowing from the crown of my head reaching to my finger-tips, slipping between my legs to the soles of my feet

To be in thought of you

is most powerful

celebrating a state of mindfulness

with you intertwining

my spirit with your twin spirit

surging energy throughout my entire body with only the expansion of my consciousness reaching out to your name

your name

to say your name fully awakens me, tunneling to my very core

in waves, transmuting from my lower chakra to my heart, illuminating a divine union with you

To be in thought with you is sacred.

The most spiritual essence of you lifts to my crown

as my mouth parts in heavy moans, sensations grow, sensing you tightly gripping me, calling me,

caught in the rapture of your embrace

I am safe

I'm held so safely, vibrations spreading to my hands and whispering kisses to my neck.

I moan, arching my back,

freeing myself,

granting your entrance as if you were present in time

it's so delicious

you in thought is so delicious

TO BE in thought with you

transforms my being into another place, feeling your breath trace ever so lightly down my face. I release a tear as your invisible force centers the planets.

I tremble as tingles burst from within as you gently trace your breath to my neck.

I release a cry as you center the stars.

My arms faintly fall so lovingly, your breath sweeps across my face so attentively that your breath trickles down to my nipples.

I twist, I turn, I release, sobbing out your name

you align the galaxies, even the light, gravitating all my senses, worshiping every aspect of me. My heart burst open; tears flow so freely

in thought of you, your arms are a beauty. so freeing, so held, so safe, so beautiful, so understood

by you

I cry, captivated by the beauty

in thought of you, I cry for I have never known such beauty, such safety, such ecstasy, and I'm only
in thought of you
moaning, crying, almost dying;
You saved me
rescued me in your invisible state
lifting me from dimensions like a secret,
your sacred messages transport me,
passing me through,
loving me,
bringing me to shivers of ecstasy
yes, it's all so seamless
in thought of you
yes
yes
beautiful
incredible
yes
yes
yes
so connected, intimately flowing
penetrating the depth of me
yes
coming and going
emotions of you
with you
intensely taken by you
yet you never have touched my face
my breath as if I just finished a race
to be with you
to be in thought of you

my my my
opens the divine within, escorting me to God
bringing me to my true self
timeless, infinite love
surging within me as an earthquake erupts
moans
cries
yells
centering me as the universe
just in thought of you.

UNEARTH ME

I woke up in heaven feeling your embrace, my lips turning up as energy shifts
tingling from my arms
My eyes meet the golden sun rays peeking through the shade
vibrations
waves internally
You have a way of unearthing me
Unblocking my tear ducts so I may see
What's been hidden from me
The fire of your words eliminates all stampedes
elevating my soul
as you
Chaperon me to Be
Living as a tiger among sheep
You give me food,
You unearth me

Me…the tiger feasting as a sheep in an illusion trapped from the reality of my father's words,

"I am full of potential."

You unearth me

Transforming from the death of an old form

You unearth me

Rebirthing me with affection, patience

like a teacher with his student

removed from tension

You unearth me

Rebirthing me as I experience being alive

With you before my eyes,

it's like a rebirth of love

Precious

Rebirth where the road only leads to increasing after a decline.

Where weeds grew amidst, encasing my rich

Telling me, I am not

I can't

I won't

Constantly telling me myths

You give me food

You unearth me

Returning me to my rich origins as gold richer than gold

Reminding me of my golden connection of knowing

Knocking the stone, encoded with material reflecting the image of union yet solo my existence…a stone that's blemished my gold

Yet before my eyes

You
Rebirth love
Unearthing me to bliss
My authentic journey,
bliss, my serenity…unearthing me to bliss.

ANEW

The memory of your smile fills me with radiating shades of orange and pink, inviting me to a new day.

I FEEL a tingly sensation of your invisible fingers lifting my foot and pushing strokes toward my upper thighs.

I sigh, relaxing as you are the gentle passion of my soul.

YOUR VERY ESSENCE escorts me home, untangling the fragile beginnings of affection.

EVEN AS I whisper your name, it's as if honey drips from my lips.

. . .

SHUTTING MY EYES, I breathe in, meeting your eyes, locked with mine, seeing galaxies of possibilities.

YOU SEE me through rose-colored glasses; your acceptance of me empowers me.

SAYING YOUR NAME, I gain spiritual chills from the top of my head, spreading to the depth of my toes.

A VALIDATION of truth reveals the moment I exclaim your name again, and my lower lips pulsate.

I GASP for air as my worries loosen, reframing from resistance the world seems to stop yet still on the axis.

No sound,
No wind,
No time…free to the love I prayed for.

SEEING you snatches the breath from my lungs,

You have a certain life in your eyes staring toward me,
telling me I'm a rarest breed,

HOLDING eye contact longer than necessary, reminding me how precious I am as I revert to childlike form.

AS YOUR STRONG arms transmit messages to

my body, brain, and soul... you are with me,
I revert to a childlike form.

CHEEK TO CHEEK, I mentally confess I love you; my words escape, for longing for your presence is like a crisis, for it has a way of making me a mere silhouette, yearning to be touched by your skin.

IN YOUR EMBRACE, the world melts away; my muscles loosen, my optimism rises as I feel cherished, cradled in your arms.

Anew I feel
Cherished
Anew I feel

WITH YOUR BLESSING, I brush my fingers upon your face.

. . .

CARESSING the gentleness of your skin, I convey how special and tender you are to me.

I wish an exchange of peace unto you

as I mentally profess my love to you,
my heart races, empowered by our being.

THOUGH OUR PHYSICAL state is not present

your essence remains deeply within me as
the start of a new day is such bliss!

STARVATION

Your vibrations set off a mission of resuscitation of my being in starvation.

YOUR SPIRIT INTERTWINING with my spirit has been an awakening…

LOOKING at my yesterday
a glimpse from moments and writings from my past
where a prescription was written
yet I never filled
to begin the healing process
to secure my survival
as I roamed life, existing
is more like an optical illusion

for my severe acute malnutrition prevention treatment took place
between the time our energies embraced.

FALLING APART, like tissue paper upon the windshield in the rain, an emergency therapeutic transformation took place with your words,
glance,
touch,
it has all been surreal.

TO KNOW I was starving that instance, my palate gasped, the mere breath you breathe is the day a rebirth spiraling within supervened.

I DO NOT LOOK BACK at yesterday
to be my future
for it is a death and my rebirth
to live
to be
to love
Is all before me as the ascending angels cheer me on
delights of my decision to take provisions to manifest my life, after death parade, my existence.

MY FIGHT in life has not been a resolution to change one, but many.

. . .

YOU HAVE BEEN a transfusion to me
and yet many more
for you yielding to resurrect me,
stabilize my equilibrium,
streamline my famine relief...
Fine-tuning me gingerly to be
Is a gift from the gods to be.

YOUR VIBRATIONS SET off a mission of resuscitation of my being in starvation.

I'M SO pleased the deficiency of inanition is now only part of my imagination…
farewell to who I used to be
I am who I am to Be!

ONE DAY

One day someone will gasp at the mere sight of you

Seeing you will snatch the breath from someone's lungs,

Your very essence will escort them home, untangling the fragile beginnings of affection.

The thought of you will heighten sensations, saturating inside, flowing from the crown of their head reaching to their fingertips, slipping between their legs, to the soles of their feet

Cheek to cheek, mentally confessing your love

. . .

REALIZING they have been in starvation, their pallet gasps
the mere breath you breathe

SEEING you as a transfusion
and yet much more
for you yield to resurrect them,
stabilizing their equilibrium,
streamlining their famine relief...

ONE DAY

ACKNOWLEDGMENTS

I am grateful to the following people for their support:

My heart, my inspiration, myself, I thank myself for enduring the many changes, supporting my dreams, and helping me remain focused. Through the death of my mother, I have learned to dream like I have never known an obstacle. Through the beginning of a new chapter in life, I have become aware of my true strength, overcoming the most challenging aspects has introduced me to my true self.

Thank you, Trescina, Jabari, Dean, Bryan, Willie, LaDarryl, Cameron, Zeus, Totteanna, Michael, Dwight, my children and my parents for believing in me when I could not believe in myself. It is through your words I found the courage to truly live.

Thank you Trescina Bell, Kietha Besok, and YoVonda Coleman for being a constant reminder towards the publishing of my stories. Your persistence and support is amazing.

Thank you, Lydia Moore for being caring, understanding, and supportive. You remain most gentle with me when writing has been challenging. You have a way with reminding me of my mother's words: *Never Stop Writing*

ABOUT THE AUTHOR

Dr. J. Bliss resides in Georgia, influenced by, Maya Angelo, Toni Morrison, Terry McMillan, and her own mother's writing, Dr. J began writing stimulating poetry at the age of thirteen. She dreamt of being an author and never gave up on the passion deep to write that she held within herself.

Education Dr. J. Bliss is a certified relationship, intimacy, and trauma awareness coach. She has attained a Doctorate in English from Murray State University. A graduate of Clayton State University with a Master's in English. Additionally, she has a Master's degree in Education from Troy University, a Bachelor's degree in Journalism from the University of Central Oklahoma, and an Associate's degree in Journalism from Rose State College. Her hobbies include reading, writing, teaching, event planning, and drawing.

Thank you for reading *The Cadence of My Heart.* Please leave a review. It would be most appreciated! Be sure to check out more books by Dr. J. Bliss.

-Stalk Dr. J.

ALSO BY DR. J BLISS

The Cadence of my Heart: Renewal

The Cadence of my Heart: Moving On

The Evolution of Me

Chance Series Titles by J Bliss

Not By Chance

Taking Chances

Last Chance

Breaking Dance

No Chance

Additional Titles

Perfect, Imperfect Christmas Vol. I

Perfect, Imperfect Christmas Vol. II

No "I Do" in my Future Vol. III

"I Do" in my Future Vol. IV

Night and Day: Sr. Rodd

Your Chance: Hunted

Legal Chances

J Bliss Books Publishing Company

Atlanta, GA USA

www.jblissbooks.com

Cover Design Jamila Pamoja-Thomas & Cameron Wilson;

Cover Photographer **Kauwuane Burton**;

Art Direction Cameron Wilson & Jamila Pamoja-Thomas

www.ingramcontent.com/pod-product-compliance
Lightning Source LLC
Chambersburg PA
CBHW042338150426
43195CB00001B/36
9781732772489